Mondays with Myrtle

Rosemary Ward Laberee

MONDAYS WITH MYRTLE

Published by Rebel Magic Books
www.rebelmagicbooks.com

To contact the author, visit: www.rebelmagicbooks.com

ISBN: 9781686588365

To Myrtle

Contents

To All Seniors

All the boys are singing sad songs
They forgot Sweet Adaline,
Those nursing homes are breaking up that
old gang of mine.

There goes Jack, there goes Jill ~~there~~ their over
the hill
Now and then we meet again and I
forget and call him Phil.

Oh I get a lonely feeling when the day
turns into night,
I know the stars are shining but they
don't seem quite so bright.

When I go out walking it's just not
the same
I spend my time just talking as I
lean on my cane

~~You know~~ The world is going crazy
Some say it's cause of us.
That we are always nagging and causing
such a fuss.
Now I wish that I could stay around and
set the record straight.
But the casino bus is here now and the
driver he won't wait.
See God Bless my buddies God Bless my
friends sooner or later we'll all meet again

M.L. Ward 6/2000

To All Seniors

All the boys are singing sad songs,
they forgot Sweet Adeline.
Those nursing homes are breaking up that
old gang of mine.
There goes Jack, there goes Jill
they're over the hill
Now and then we meet again and
I forget and call him Phil.

Oh I get a lonely feeling when the day
turns into night.
I know the stars are shining but they
don't seem quite so bright.
When I go out walking, it's just not
the same
I spend my time just talking as I
lean on my cane.
The world is going crazy
some say it's cause of us.
That we are always nagging and causing
such a fuss.
Now, I wish that I could stay around and
Set the record straight.
But the casino bus is here now and the
driver he won't wait.
Soooo God Bless my buddies
God bless my friends
Sooner or later, we'll all meet again.

Hope is the thing with feathers
That perches in the soul
And sings the tune without the words
And never stops – at all

Emily Dickinson

Introduction

This book is part memoir and part dementia survival guide.

For those of you too horror-struck to ask, it seeks to answer these questions:

How will death come?

What will it look like?

How long will it take?

Terrible questions with only sad answers.

Chances are you are reading this because your life has been touched and changed by someone's dementia – probably a parent, a grandparent, or a spouse. You are afraid, stunned and exhausted. You are searching, for practical advice, hope, and someone who understands your loss. Maybe a place to sit and weep. Welcome.

I am not a doctor nor am I any kind of medical professional or scientist. I am your average person – *Mrs Anybody USA*. I have a husband and four children; two college grads, one starting college, and one a high school sophomore. I have bills to pay and all of the everyday worries most of us experience.

I watched my mother die of dementia. It took over ten years. She suffered.

Many times, bearing witness to her slow-motion vanishing threatened to extinguish the light in my life. It utterly flattened me. I learned some things. Chief among them was how to hold onto life's light in the midst of dementia's darkness.

I wish I'd had something to prepare me for this, something that could have offered a glimpse into how our sweet mom was actually going to die. She had dementia. This we knew. But no one ever uttered predictive words of reality. (First *x* will happen, followed by *y* and then finally *z*.) This felt unfair. If you have cancer, doctor's give you a treatment plan and expectancy for recovery or a timeline for death. This gives you a sense of control, even if that sense of control is pure folly; it is better than an interminable nothing at all.

Doctors are reluctant to tell you exactly what to expect with dementia. They equivocate.

I try hard not to do that in this book. You have been warned.

I will also shed some light on the important difference between death in old age – which is not unexpected – and the slow, incremental death of all of someone's knowing. They are not the same thing. The death by a thousand unknowings – the piece-by-piece dismantlement of personhood – is not a natural death in old age. Its impact on loved ones leaves a sorrowful mix of loss, regret, guilt and relief. In sharing Myrtle's story, I hope to reach others who find themselves thrust onto this battlefield and help them wrap their minds around it, preparing as best they can. And I hope I can help you forgive yourself the things you could not do and be grateful for the things you could.

My mother had vascular dementia. **We think.** She was never thoroughly tested; it was her gerontologist's best guess. There was nothing else wrong with her. She did not have diabetes or heart disease or cancer or high blood pressure. Which is why her decline and even her death were so prolonged. She was otherwise healthy.

Vascular dementia is one of several different types of dementia. **What is dementia, exactly?**

From the National Institute on Aging:

Dementia is the loss of cognitive functioning—thinking, remembering, and reasoning—and the loss of behavioral abilities to such an extent that it interferes with a person's daily life and activities.

Dementia is not a normal part of aging. Many people live into their 90s and beyond without any signs of dementia. The causes of dementia can vary, depending on the types of brain changes that may be taking place. Alzheimer's Disease is the most common cause of dementia in older adults. Other dementias include Lewy body dementia, frontotemporal disorders, and vascular dementia. It is common for people to have mixed dementia—a combination of two or more types of dementia.

Often people wonder, **is Alzheimer's dementia or is dementia Alzheimer's?** Good question. Simply put, Alzheimer's is one disease which causes the symptoms of dementia. Dementia is the outcome of that disease.

Dementia is the result of abnormal neurodegenerative process(es).

At the time of this writing, the 2019 Alzheimer's Association International Conference was taking place. Unlike previous years, the focus was not treatment options or drugs. The focus this year was prevention.

While there is no proven cure or treatment for Alzheimer's, a large body of research now strongly suggests that combining healthy habits promotes good brain health and reduces your risk of cognitive decline, said Maria C. Carrillo, PhD, the Alzheimer's Association's chief science officer. *The research reported today at AAIC gives us attainable, actionable recommendations that can help us all live a healthier life.*

Five research studies reported at AAIC 2019 suggest:[1]

- Adopting four or five healthy lifestyle factors reduced risk of Alzheimer's dementia by 60% compared to adopting none or only one factor.
- Adherence to a healthy lifestyle may counteract genetic risk for Alzheimer's disease.
- Having a higher cognitive reserve, built through formal education and cognitive stimulation, may benefit

---

[1] https://www.alz.org/aaic/releases_2019/sunLIFESTYLE-jul14.asp

the aging brain by reducing risk of dementia among people exposed to high levels of air pollution.

- Confirmation that early adult to mid-life smoking may be associated with cognitive impairment at mid-life, as early as one's 40s.
- Alcohol abuse significantly increased risk of dementia in older women.

With a history of failures like this with drug trials, it is little wonder that lifestyle changes are taking a front seat.

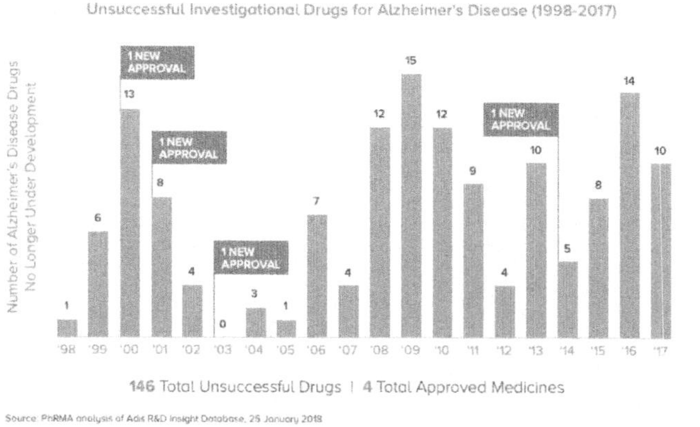

This book is not about how to prevent or cure or halt the disease in its tracks. That is left to the scientists and physicians. This book is about my own experience. It is about how dementia takes the life of someone you love and what you can do to protect your own spirit as you continue to love and care for this perishing person.

The caged bird sings with a fearful trill
of things unknown but longed for still
and his tune is heard on the distant hill
for the caged bird sings of freedom.

Maya Angelou

1
Broken Minds and Caged Birds

When I was young my family had a bird. In a cage. His name was Bingo. He never seemed to remember that he was in a cage, so every morning when we removed the night cover, Bingo flapped futilely against the thin prison bars, until he grew tired and gave up. Throughout the day, that bird sang. It sang and sang and sang. I always thought that Bingo only sang when he was happy, when he forgot that he was in a cage.

But maybe he hadn't forgotten that. What if he wasn't singing? What if he was screaming?

Myrtle is in hospice and I have converted my dining room into a bedroom for her, and Bingo keeps coming to mind.

Myrtle talks ceaselessly about going home. I don't know what to do. She resolves to go there at least fifty times a day. Earlier this week she tried to puzzle out how she would get to central Philadelphia. It went like this:

I can take a train to center city, can't I? Does a train run past this hotel? (She is referring to my home, deep in the Pine Barren woods of New Jersey.)

What will you do when you get to Philadelphia, Mom?

Go to my home.

How will you get to your home?

I'll take a bus.

But, Mom, you live here. You don't have a home in Philadelphia. (Starting to feel a bit exasperated.)

I have to have a home there!

Why?

Because that's where the bus goes.

Right. Hey, let's build something with these blocks. Watch me.

And I show Myrtle how the tangram blocks can be arranged to make any shape in the world. I don't explain *why* she lives in the suburbs of New Jersey with me or why she hasn't had a home in Philadelphia for many years. I learned my lesson weeks ago. Now, I no longer attempt to mend the holes in her consciousness.

She starts to move the pieces. Slowly, ever so slowly. It is hard for her, but she concentrates on it for a while and I clean up my kitchen, fold laundry, and get James (age 14) to do his Latin homework. When I come back, she shows me what she made.

Pretty cool, Mom. What is it?

It's a bird. It's a lucky bird.

Yep, that's a bird alright. I'm impressed! Why is it lucky?

Are you kidding me? It has wings. It can fly.

Myrt made a tangram block bird. A perfect bird. Myrtle notices birds. She enjoys watching them. My husband put a bird feeder by the window of her bedroom (aka former dining room) and in between her dozing-off and her uncontrollable weeping and her incessant questions about finding her parents, she watches the little customers that come to nibble. The eastern bluebird is her favorite. Maybe she is imagining their immense freedom.

I wonder if she longs for her youth, when she was as nimble of mind and body. I wonder if she thinks about her life before her wings were clipped and her feet were bound by this ghastly descent which consumes her soul piece by piece each day. I wonder if birds are her spirit animal.

As I was settling her into bed tonight, she called out in a shrill, frightened and plaintive voice. "Wait, wait, Rosemary!" Her face was pale and her eyes were terror-struck. "I'm afraid to drive the car", her voice quivered. "I'll need someone to drive me to the train. Okay?"

"Sure, Mom. Don't worry. I'll drive you. Everything's okay. Everything's good." Her head fell back in relief and she began the soft recitations and wailings which precede her sleep. It is a kind of singing. Whimsical intonations. A lonely lullaby. Her bird song, maybe.

Dementia is a brutal opponent. It takes and it takes, and what it leaves behind is not enough to satisfy. Where can you find some small crumbs of satisfaction? How can you move forward when it all seems so pointless?

Myrtle has no memory of the visits, the flowers, or the gifts her five children and ten grandchildren have showered upon her over the past decade. In her hijacked, broken and glaciated mind, those snapshots of delight are now invisible. The heart has a different operating system, though. The heart knows what the mind cannot. Your efforts, your kindnesses, and your gifts are like yesterday's sunshine. Gone today. But they matter. They store a different kind of value and strength. The heart stores these things. Remember that.

When a loved one's mind is pierced with this permafrost of forgetting, you have brief, imperfect moments – in between their hallucinations, rage, confusion, grief and psychosis – of recognition, gratitude and pleasure. These moments, however flawed and fragmented, truly matter. They are glimpses of the value of yesterday's sunshine. Seize them and say thank you. Let them fuel you. Because the moment will pass very quickly.

He clasps the crag with crooked hands;
Close to the sun in lonely lands,
Ring'd with the azure world, he stands.
The wrinkled sea beneath him crawls;
He watches from his mountain walls,
And like a thunderbolt he falls.

The Eagle, Alfred Lord Tennyson

2
Before the Fall

Myrtle was a fiercely independent and quick-witted woman. She was small but mighty – an energizer bunny, philosopher, comedienne, warrior, nurturer, cook, survivor, mother of five, and my daily reminder that every oak tree was once an acorn that held its ground.

I am one of her five children. We each did what we could during her many years of decline. My sister Kathleen and my brother Brian did the most, but we all did our best to shoulder the pain and the burden.

Myrtle was widowed in 1983, when she was 57. Starting in the late 1970s, and through the 1980s, her five kids moved out. Myrtle stayed in her tiny row home in the blue-collar Philadelphia neighborhood where we had all been raised. As she approached seventy, and the many steps leading to the front door of our matchbox home became tedious for her to manage, she moved a few blocks away to a modest apartment my brother Brian owned. He kept it up for her, checked in on her regularly, and promptly cleared snow and ice. This was a great arrangement, and we all visited often, grandchildren in tow.

Myrtle's confusion and forgetfulness began in earnest around age seventy-five. All five of us wondered what was happening to her, but mostly we laughed it off. It was almost endearing, the way she'd get confused and forget things. We did not know. **We did not know.**

She continued to live in the apartment until she was approaching eighty. By then, it was evident she was at risk and should not be alone. She left burners on. She began repeating questions many times over. She was skipping meals. We got Myrtle to a gerontologist for evaluation.

She was diagnosed with vascular dementia. My sister Kathleen, bless her heart, moved Mom into her own home in the suburbs of Philadelphia.

Mom enjoyed her time with my sister. She loved the dog and she loved being near her grandchildren. Kathleen often took mom to the casinos in Atlantic City and Myrtle cherished these outings. However, after five years and a few falls, a different Myrtle was emerging. She was suspicious and often belligerent. She refused to shower. We were not prepared for these stages; no one talked to us about this. **We did not know**.

She suffered from frequent and debilitating anxiety attacks, and the medication for this left her too wobbly to walk. We all knew that she could not, and should not, be left alone, not even for an hour. The job had become too big, even for my big-hearted sister.

Brian, Susan, and I began to search for a place for Mom to live. She did not have much money, so the fancy retirement homes with memory care units that we visited were not an option. We also visited the dimly lit, poorly-funded facilities which smelled of sadness, urine, and death. Although within budget these were utterly unacceptable.

We were all stretched thin. We were all busy with our lives. Just finding the time to look at different facilities was a burden. Add to this the not knowing, and the inability to conjure up a timeline and best/worst case scenario plans. It was hard on all of us. We were always in a reactive state, scrambling against a fog of unknowing – our own and Myrtle's.

While we were searching for a place for Mom, over and over again I thought: *how is this story going to end? How does a person with dementia actually die? This is getting really hard to manage.* ***What's going to happen next?*** *Does dementia make your heart stop beating eventually?* ***How does this work?***

These are dreadful thoughts, but they're normal. Death by dementia came by degrees, taking and taking and taking from Mom, until there was no more to take. Until she simply forgot how to stay alive.

It might not unfold this way for you and your loved one. Many other factors and conditions can end their suffering. No one wishes for this but everyone wants to limit the anguish of this unbearably slow loss.

There are some wonderful Facebook groups you can join. (See **Resources** at the end of this book.) Everyone is in the same situation in these groups. No question is considered too personal or too clinical. Sometimes, the answers will be hard to hear, but they will be heartfelt and honest. People will connect with you on an intimate, human level almost immediately. You will instantly become a comrade – you are fighting in the same war.

You broke your wing; it dragged the land
And etched your mark upon the sand.
When feathers break, you cannot fly,
But who decides the time to die?

Delia Owens

3
My Mondays with Myrtle

It took a few weeks and many miles in the minivan, but we lucked out in our search for a place for Mom. We found a home in the Philadelphia neighborhood where Myrtle had lived and raised a family. Skeptical, I visited. The *Roxborough Home for Women* was a perfect fit for Mom. It wasn't a memory care facility but most of the women living there were in some stage of dementia. They didn't have nursing care, but Mom didn't need that. Yet.

Even at this stage, we didn't know the path ahead. Nursing? What would a nurse do exactly? What would happen to our dear mother that she'd need an attendant nurse? We were in a reactive state with no clear vision of the last few legs of Mom's journey.

The home had rules. In order to stay, Mom had to be ambulatory. She was. She had to be able to dress and feed herself. She could. She had to be able to shower and use the bathroom without assistance. She could. They accepted her.

The facility dispensed all medications. We were very grateful for this, as Myrtle could not be trusted with this task. They had a weekly hairdressing appointment for each of the ladies living there. Sweet. They had parties on all major holidays. The food was decent, her room was warm in the winter and cool in the summer, and the building was surrounded by flowers and trees. Mom moved in two weeks later.

I would visit Mom once a week, usually Mondays. It was a long drive from my place in New Jersey to the Home, and I wished I could do it more than once a week, but my kids still needed me. The discomfort caused by this squeeze on my time, in middle age, was intense. **It is the most common, bone-wearying complaint of those caring for an elderly parent.**

My Mondays with Myrtle were the good days, although I didn't know it at the time.

Although Myrtle was confused most of the time, she was able to walk and she participated in all the Home's parties and events. She made friends easily. She always had. She ambled around from room to room, enjoying time on the porch and in the community TV room. Myrt was a very funny lady. Always cracking jokes, she found humor in everything. She always smiled. They liked her. She had one very good friend who was her doppelganger, Louise.

I was visiting with Mom in her little room when I met Louise. She strolled in, all ninety pounds of her, and my mom introduced me as Susan, my youngest sister. I didn't bother to correct her. Louise beamed and told me how much she loved Myrtle. As she chattered on cheerily, she urinated with surprising force and generosity right through her doll-sized grey slacks, creating a neat puddle at her feet. Mom, sitting in her rocker not two yards away, didn't notice. They both wore Mardi Gras necklaces that they toyed with. They kept laughing and smiling. I tried, with some effort, not to react to the puddle on the floor. After all, Louise did not seem to know she had peed a quart onto the carpet, and Mom didn't know either. I was the only one who missed a few beats in the festive little chat we were having. These two lady friends were so happy in each other's company, they either didn't notice or they didn't care. That taught me something.

After she had been at the Home for a couple of years, one of the staff confided in me that Mom wept bitterly for hours after I left each week. I don't know why the staff member told me this, because it broke me a little. It reached back in time and took away the joy I had stored there from being a caring daughter visiting every week. And it reached ahead and made me anxious about future visits. I don't think the staff person meant any harm; I think she thought she was being helpful. **You do not want or need to hear everything.** Sometimes it is better if staff don't overshare things like this.

Mom lived happily at the Home for five years. In the first year, she had a phone in her room. But she started calling Brian and Kathleen constantly. She never called me or Daniel or Susan. None of us knows how she made her choices in this behavior, but she was relentless. She'd call them at all hours, crying and demanding to be let out of prison. My poor siblings would call the front desk at the Home and they'd quickly send an aide to check on Mom. She would either be sleeping or she'd have no memory of the calls.

We disconnected the phone. She continued calling but the calls went nowhere. Myrtle never realized this. Sometimes when I visited her, she'd be talking on the phone. She thought there was someone on the other end, but I could see that it wasn't plugged in.

Oh well.

Mondays with Myrtle continued, and so did her steady decline. She could not remember the names of her grandchildren. She did not know where she was, how she got there, or how long she had been there. Every time I visited, she would tell me she had just arrived at this Home and wasn't planning to stay. "*This place is okay, but I'm leaving tomorrow. My father is waiting for me.*" Her father died fifty years ago. She never wanted me to leave, but I had a long, arduous drive back. It took over an hour to get there and could be longer if I got stuck in traffic. The hardest part of visiting was walking away, knowing that she had only a child's grasp on time, if that. And now I also knew she cried after I left. This is when I took comfort in the fact that she didn't remember things. At all. This applied to good things and bad things. She'd soon forget I was there, so she'd soon stop crying, I told myself.

She never remembered my visits. Every week when she saw me, she asked why I so rarely visited. It was useless to object or explain, information was like wisps of smoke, vanishing in seconds. And she became agitated if I gently told her that I had visited last week. Often, she responded angrily, "*No, you have not visited me in years, I'd remember that!*" That was the experience she was having and that's the only thing that matters in this strange life with dementia. I learned that peace of mind was relative. It was going to come from me, from the inside. There was nothing about my outward life with Myrtle that offered me peace of mind. It really was an inside job.

Often Myrtle forgot who I was halfway through my visit. She'd sit smiling at me politely, and I could see in her eyes that I'd become a stranger.

I always took her for a walk. She couldn't walk on concrete, so she used a wheelchair outside and the home permitted it, despite their rule about no wheelchairs. I'd wheel her up and down Leverington Avenue and sometimes down Ridge Avenue and she'd marvel over how things had changed. God, how she enjoyed those walks! They were a gift to her, and now to me, as I cherish the memories of the wonder on her face. She knew this neighborhood!

She knew the streets. She knew the area. The geography was embedded in her long-term memory in a space the dementia hadn't reached. This neighborhood – her childhood neighborhood, my childhood neighborhood – was fully intact.

"Woolworths was in that building there, Rosemary, do you remember that?" she asked one day. Wow! She knew it was me pushing the wheelchair *and* she reported a real memory!

"Yes, Mom! I do remember it. You'd let me get a *Coca-Cola* and a grilled cheese sandwich if you were in a good mood," I chided her pleasantly, although the sweet childhood memory put a lump in my throat. Myrtle giggled. "*Ha*!" she replied, conspiratorially, "*I always pretended to be in a bad mood when I didn't have enough money for that stuff*", she said, and then fell into a quiet humming. I never knew this, but it rang true. And it flattened me. I let myself cry. She couldn't see. Just as well. It would have confused her.

In her last two years at the home, she fell a few times, resulting in hospitalizations. Although she rarely injured herself seriously, the hospital stays robbed her of the last few bits of neuro-connectivity she owned. She became unhinged. Lost. Cognitively stranded. It was written in her eyes and on the lines of her face. She'd recognize someone or something and try desperately to hold on, but these touch downs were fleeting. It was brutal witnessing a temporary relief wash over her, only to see it quickly displaced by abject terror.

No one prepared us for the hospital losses. An elderly person in the grips of dementia pays a heavy toll in a hospital bed. **Hospitals are kryptonite for the cognitively challenged.**

Hospitalizations disoriented her fragile grip on reality, and they made her physically weak. Until they were sure she was stable, the staff would keep her in bed for two or three days, and during this time she'd lose the strength, balance, and desire to stand. She would forget how to stand up.

After her last hospitalization in 2016, she lost the ability to stand and walk and the Home said she had to leave. This was the end of Mondays with Myrtle. It was also the beginning of the hardest phase of her decline.

It is your job to remember the good you do your loved one when you visit. Congratulate yourself for every visit, for every act of selflessness and love. Find your own comfort in doing the right thing in spending time with them. They might accuse you of abandonment. They might not remember your visits. **This is something you must laugh off or shrug off.** Do something kind in each visit. Comb her hair, help him shave, rub lotion on her hands and arms, bring a favorite treat. Do this for yourself, for your memory of the visit. Your loved one will have a fleeting moment of pleasure when you give this gift, then it will be gone. But you will have the memory of this gift for years to come. I have learned how much this matters.

But a caged bird stands on the grave of dreams
his shadow shouts on a nightmare scream
his wings are clipped and his feet are tied
so he opens his throat to sing.

Maya Angelou

4

Homeless and in Hospice

After her last fall in 2016, Myrtle was released from the hospital and we took her back to the Home, although we knew it was only for a short time. Her doctor placed her on hospice. **None of us understood what this meant.** *Is she dying, now? I wondered. Can I ask the doctor this question? Will she think I am an ogre? Am I an ogre for needing to know more?*

The Home was emphatic when Myrtle returned from her last hospital visit – they could not care for her now. We had two weeks to find a place for Myrtle to live. All of her children had jobs and demanding lives. Who doesn't? The search began.

Myrtle was eighty-nine. She could no longer walk. She could not bath herself or get onto a toilet without help. She needed assistance dressing and she sometimes needed help feeding herself. We looked for a memory care facility. We got close to a few matches, but when they met

Myrtle, the price usually doubled. It did not take them long to see that she could not really do anything for herself.

Many places wanted a lump sum buy-in. Not possible.

Many wanted over $15,000 a month, but we knew within a few short months, Myrtle's entire savings would be gone. We became aware that facilities that take everything a poor patient owns, and then (resentfully) make do with the social security sign-over, often provide minimal care. We were skeptical and vigilant.

Other than being in the final stages of dementia, Myrtle was not unhealthy. She did not have heart disease, high blood pressure or diabetes. Terrible though it was, we came to understand that Myrtle was going to lose her life to dementia, and not something else. And that it was not going to happen quickly. We were circumspect about where she went. It could be a long stay.

I visited her the day after she had been temporarily reinstalled at the Home. She was sitting and staring at her breakfast food. The last hospital stay had taken so much from her. She was a shell of a human being but with enough wisps of humanity left to be afraid.

She wasn't clean and she wasn't happy, and it rent my heart to pieces. As she stared at the food on her plate, I realized that she had forgotten how to feed herself. I kneeled to talk with her and she beamed with joy, although I could tell she couldn't hear anything I said. Her hearing aids weren't in. I was angry. Mom was isolated by her dementia and scared all the time; not being able to hear made it worse. I searched for the hearing aids, found them, and showed them to her before I put them in her ears. If I'd just reached for her ears, she'd have been alarmed. When I held them out in my hand, she stared at them the longest time. She picked one out of my hand, looked at it closely, turning it over in her fingers, studying it. Then she ate it.

The deadline arrived for her to leave the Home, but we had no good prospects. I had discussed moving Myrtle into my home with my husband and my two teen sons. Everyone was okay with this. I was afraid. I knew enough to realize I would be stepping into an abyss, but we were between a rock and a hard place.

Since Myrtle had been placed in hospice care, we thought this meant that she would go to a new home and be cared for by nurses. It does not mean this. It means that a nurse or caregiver will visit once or twice, or possibly even three times a week, where the patient lives. They help. That's it. They will give you one or two hours of relief. They will change bedding, change diapers, and give your loved one a sponge bath. They are kind and good human beings and I was grateful for them. There was no fee for this vital help. It is covered by Medicare. However, the bulk of the care simply falls onto the family members.

I braced myself for the enormous change and prepared my family as much as I could.

My sons moved my dining room furniture downstairs and the hospice company delivered a bed and some supplies the next day. Two days after Mom tried to eat her hearing aid, my brother and I moved her into my home.

She immediately fell in love with our dog. This was the perfect distraction from the disruption of a move.

Myrtle had no idea that she had been relocated; she didn't know where she was from one hour to the next. Mercifully, she slept through the drive to my home, although she was upset on arrival.

Several times on that first day, she asked if she could return to the planet Earth. *I'd like to go back there, I think,* she mumbled it again as I was tucking her into bed, and I thought how nice it felt to be her mom, to switch roles. And, I felt an unearthly fatigue and weariness. It was a long day, and I too wanted to return to earth.

As your loved one becomes a child once again and you assume the role of parent, you will feel a bone-deep weariness. Whether you become a caregiver in your own home or a frequent visitor in someone else's home or facility, you will feel the tiredness that comes with an unnatural, suspended state of existence. You now live in the strange space between living and dying. This can be experienced as hostile shadows where your life energy gets swallowed whole.

There is nothing wrong with you. You are legitimately tired.

Your loved one hangs between the real world and a crazy quilt of some past life, and you are stuck in this ghostly cognitive waiting room, guiltily wondering how to cope and when your loved one's number will be called.

Be kind to yourself. Call friends and cry often. And remind yourself that this is a sad season, but a temporary one.

Birds are born with an instinct for flight.
But it is a skill that must be learned.
It takes practice.

5
Learning Curves

One of the hardest things about being my mother's caregiver was my own lack of sleep. Her circadian rhythms were non-existent. Sometimes she slept for many hours during the day but not at night. Sometimes she slept all through the night but would not nap during the day.

Often, when I put her to bed around 8pm, she didn't go to sleep. Sleep was unpredictable. She woke often and wanted to get out of bed at midnight or 2am. She often got up at daybreak, around 5:30am. If I didn't appear by her side immediately, she would yell and yell and yell for help and everyone in the house would be disturbed. I was fragile and foggy from the lack of sleep.

I had much to learn about Myrtle.

First lesson: removing her teeth. False teeth cannot be extracted from an unwilling mouth. This I learned quickly. Myrtle had developed a problem with her gums and her doctor had asked me to be certain she took her dentures out before going to bed. Not an easy task. She argued vociferously against removing her dentures. *"You will lose them",* she insisted, and she sealed her lips like a two-year-old. She lived in fear of losing her teeth. She had lost them for days at a time in the past few years. They'd show up under the base of a lamp or inside a plant or in a trash can. She'd hide them. No one knows why, but she did.

She would not let me soak her teeth in *Efferdent*; she wouldn't part with them. In exasperation, I suggested that I would take out my teeth too, and we could soak our teeth together. She liked this idea.

I don't wear dentures.

But my teenage sons had fake teeth from a Halloween costume, and I placed these in a glass with an *Efferdent* tablet. I showed it to her. She smiled and promptly took out her teeth and dropped them in. That was it. I went through this charade every night and it worked every time.

My second lesson was with her eyeglasses. Five years prior, Mom had had laser surgery correcting her distance vision. Before that, she'd worn thick glasses her whole life, and with the onset of her dementia she was constantly losing them. Corrective surgery was the solution to this, and it also helped her be fully present more often. Before the surgery, if she couldn't find her glasses, she was visually stranded, alongside being hearing impaired and cognitively impaired. When she first moved in to my house, all of a sudden she wanted her glasses. She asked for them constantly. I had them, but the lenses had popped out. They were merely empty frames. Broken, empty frames.

Why do you want your glasses?

I can't see. I need my glasses!

But you don't need glasses, Mom.

Get my glasses, dammit. I can't see!

I would leave the room and get the empty frames from a bag of costume jewelry and bric-a-brac. Mom would grab them with great relief and put them on.

There ya go. Now I can see!

She believed she could see better with the empty frames on her face. She was happy and satisfied. I did not understand the rules of this game and I was not very good at it.

My third lesson was the most difficult. Mom moved in with bags and bags of *Depends*. For days she told me she didn't need to wear these. She'd been wearing *Depends* for the last three years. She would often smell ripe because she needed a change.

Once she moved in with me, I changed her *Depends* several times a day. This meant getting my mom on and off the toilet several times a day. It involved heavy lifting and slow, arduous maneuverings in the bathroom. Each and every time, her *Depends* was dry and she would void her bladder into the toilet. She was right. She did not need to wear a diaper.

I stopped insisting and bought her lots of new underwear. She had no accidents at all for almost a month. But then she did, and it was traumatic. It required many hours of clean-up. I shared my regrettable decision with the hospice workers. They smiled knowingly and suggested using the *Depends*, and never second guess it. An entire room can be destroyed by one accident. When we went back to the *Depends*, Mom would still tell me she didn't need them. I would agree with her and then change her into a fresh one, whether she needed it or not. It felt like a defeat, but it was not the worst defeat. That was yet to come.

Blackbird singing in the dead of night,
Take these sunken eyes and learn to see.
All your life, you were only waiting for this moment to be free.

The Beatles

6
No Rules

Myrtle had a Mickey Mouse wrist watch. The plastic cover was missing, broken many years ago, and it had no hands. She loved it.

Several times a day, Myrtle asked the time. Like a record stuck on one phrase, this question replayed throughout every day. I would look at my smart phone and give her a correct answer. Every. Single. Time.

"Do you want tea or coffee mom? I'm making myself some coffee."

"That depends. What time is it?" she replies, thoughtfully.

"It's 9:30 in the morning," I say.

Myrtle consults her watch. *"No way. That contraption* (my iPhone) *is wrong. Look, it's noon,"* she says impatiently pointing at the handless Mickey, *"We have to go, I'm gonna be late."*

This was a familiar dance. Usually, she would move her wheelchair toward the front door and try to get out of it. She always forgot that she could no longer walk. I would try to distract her with a task – sometimes this worked, sometimes it did not. Often, I'd go along with her need to leave, pushing her over the threshold of my front door for a walk up and down the driveway in her wheelchair.

Rain or shine. We ground a rut into that driveway. She loved these walks. She especially loved the rainy ones; the drizzle on her sneakers made her laugh out loud. Once outside, Myrtle usually forgot that she had other intentions. We'd stroll up and down the hill three or four times. Back inside, she would often ask where she was and how long she would be "in this hotel." I didn't correct her.

"Just a little while longer," I'd say.

"But where are all the people?" she'd always ask, genuinely confused.

I had no answer and offered none.

"What time is it?" she barked.

"It's 10 am, Mom".

She consulted Mickey, the amputee.

"What? No way. It's 8 o'clock, look!", she'd tap Mickey emphatically. *"It's time for bed! I'm going home to my father tomorrow; he's waiting for me."*

"Sounds like a plan, Mom."

It is stressful operating every hour of every day in a fake world. Surprisingly stressful.

Although you will witness a steady decline, you will also experience things which defy explanation. How does someone, who doesn't know where she is and doesn't grasp that her wristwatch is no different than a silent bracelet, win a game of cards?

One day my 14-year-old found a deck of cards and asked Myrtle to play a game of War. "Don't worry Mom, I'll let Grandmom win," he said to me, magnanimously.

Not only did Myrtle stay fully engaged through the entire game, but she caught him making mistakes twice and she completely demolished him. Not kidding. War is a simple game, but it was an impressive feat for someone in her late stage of cognitive decline. Right after this game, we went for one of our walks up and down the driveway in her wheelchair. She pointed into the woods at a dense grouping of pine trees and oddly enough she 'saw' the house she grew up in. *"Oh, there's my old home on Umbria Street,"* she reported, sharply. She grew up in the Manayunk section of Philadelphia, which is many miles away.

"That's wonderful, Mom!" I replied, peeking under her sun hat to find her eyes closed. She was smiling.

Myrtle often had her eyes closed, although she was fully awake. I asked her gerontologist about this and she showed some concern. Some people suffering from dementia forget how to open their eyes, she explained. Something turns off this automatic function.

Ah. Here is a useful piece of information, I thought. So, I gathered up my courage and asked, *is that what will happen to Myrtle? Will her brain just gradually forget how to do each and every little thing?*

But all of my searches for cold hard facts like this were gently pushed aside with equivocations. "Well, it depends. Possibly, but not necessarily. Every person is different. But try to help her keep her eyes open. That would be better for her."

Maybe, I thought. But, maybe not. Maybe she's connecting to a memory so fragile that everything else has to be blocked out so she can hold onto that photograph in her mind, unchallenged, without the fog and confusion. I wasn't at all sure that I should try to keep Myrtle's eyes open during the day, but I did as the doctor said.

It is alarming to watch someone talk to you, fidget with a blanket, and even try to eat, without ever opening their eyes. But I think I understood it. I think she wass concentrating more when her eyes were closed.

Sadly, I became afraid that her closed eyes would become permanent, leaving Myrtle blind *and* deaf *and* in the advanced stages of cognitive decline. I combatted this by introducing her to a scratch and draw art book. She really liked it. Remarkably, she remembered how to draw. More remarkably, she drew a bird, and drew it well. With her eyes closed.

Every time you think you know what is going on with your loved one, they will surprise you with some skill you assumed was lost long ago. Just as often, they will point to a broken clock with no hands and insist that it is offering the correct time of day. **There are no rules.**

In the midst of this uneven cognitive landscape, you are witnessing a death. A death unlike others. When someone dies of a regrettable but common disease process – cancer, heart disease, diabetes – there is a systematic downward decline. While it is obvious when someone has dementia, the timeline is not at all obvious. Some pieces of the victim's mind are left unmarred. It is just enough to keep you wondering. And hopeful.

Consequently, when there is a sudden setback, it knocks you over. You never really feel prepared for the final chapter. You are on a smooth road and you start to relax and enjoy the ride. You hit a sudden speed bump and it jolts you. You look ahead and see a brick wall and think, *This is it! This is how we die.* Except you don't, because you go through the wall and get back on smooth road again. That is a day in the life of dementia.

On days like this, I would return to the nagging, guilt-drenched thought: *What will Myrtle's death look like?*

Myrtle is old. Like all of us, on the day she was born, she began her fall toward the grave. Everything that lives must one day die. The amount of time in between birth and death will vary, but death is inevitable. This fact doesn't really trouble me. I accept it. What I can't accept are the strange methods of this particular footman of death. He is more blameworthy than others. His methods are unnatural. **He takes the personhood away before he takes the person.**

It is rare to see a dead bird on your lawn or your porch. Dead birds alarm us more than other dead animals, because they don't normally die in public. If they are out in the open, something unnatural has taken place. It is an incongruity. It is startling and unexpected. We know this instinctively and that's why it troubles us. Birds don't die on the wing. They have an instinct for dying alone.

I wonder if Myrtle will do this. It keeps me up at night, until I comfort myself with the knowledge that she is a flightless bird now. While I still have no idea how death will come, I am certain I will be with her and that she will not face it alone.

These are the days when Birds come back —
A very few — a Bird or two —
To take a backward look.

Emily Dickinson

7
Try, Try Again

A good day was a day with few tears. That's about it. When Myrtle was fully occupied, she did not cry as much. I worked hard to find ways to keep her busy. This was monumentally difficult; there are only a few things she could do. This aspect of caregiving took focus, forethought, and steely determination.

Myrtle loved her flowers. She always did. I bought a supply and variety of artificial plastic flowers and Styrofoam bricks, so that she could do flower arrangements. She liked this activity. She was surprised every time I'd pull these supplies out – she never really remembered doing it the day before. No problem. After 15 or 20 minutes of arranging, she'd sit and look at the flowers. She was probably tired of the activity but didn't know what to do about that. She'd never say *I'm tired of doing this* or *What's next?* She would instead enter a suspended state where she stopped and stared blankly into space.

This was a cue to move on. I would pull out the big picture books of flowers. Myrtle would study these big images of the rare flowers of the Pine Barrens. Some days, she stayed utterly absorbed in this activity for over an hour. That always surprised me.

I often stuck to the flower theme and would encourage her to paint flowers, and just as often this would work and more time would pass.

I even bought cups, soil and seeds so she could plant. This made her so happy. Myrtle loved gardens and gardening and she knew a lot about gardening. The neural real estate which stored her gardening knowledge stayed completely intact. She could name the species of flowers based on a photo and she was so clever with planting good seeds. She was joyful having her hands in the soil, and the memory of that afternoon will be in my heart always.

The most valuable skills Myrtle taught me are the ones I rely on so heavily, now that I am her caregiver. She was always plainspoken and blunt, with a heavy dose of eternal optimism and cheerfulness. Growing up, I had the sense that there was nothing she couldn't handle and nothing that would shock her. She was unflappable. Yet she laughed at herself often, and when life revealed its treachery, she laughed at that too. She gifted these characteristics to me, or so I am told. I called on them hourly. Sometimes they rescued me and sometimes they were not enough.

Each day with Myrtle was a cryptogram. If she was unwell in some way, it would manifest in an odd behavior because she did not experience pain directly. If she got bored, she wept and fidgeted. If she was anxious, she demanded to be taken to her parents. As with cryptograms, nothing is what it seems to be. Each day was a riddle, a brain-teaser, to be decoded. Each day was a new knot to untie.

Myrtle loved puzzles as much as she loved flowers. As a child, I can remember our family always had a 1,000-piece work-in-progress under the tablecloth of our dining room table. After dinner, she would quietly conduct an unveiling, carefully lifting the cloth, revealing the fragmented impression beneath with its many disordered bits. We would all join in. She never said, *"Come here and work on this, kids."* Nope. She simply revealed the unfinished. That was our cue to come to the table and begin the work.

In my home, and in the advanced stages of cognitive decline, she was still revealing the pieces and I was still trying to put it all together.

Of the tools in the toolbox I turned to each morning to launch our day and to get us through the unfilled hours, some were successful. These were our good days. But not every effort was successful. Some were abysmal failures.

Like this: A basic jigsaw. Simple. No more than 30 pieces. I was pleased with myself for remembering how much she loved putting things together. But it proved to be too much for her. Almost an hour went by and she just sat and stared at the pieces, picking them up and then putting them back down, perplexed. I had even lined up the outside border to make it easier. No go. I offered to help. *"Go away!"* she said angrily. It confused and embarrassed her that she could not do this basic jigsaw and it broke my heart. I had miscalculated. I put that puppy dog jigsaw away thinking I had to try again. I watched as she repeatedly folded, unfolded and refolded a paper towel. That was it. I grabbed every cloth dinner napkin and every small terry cloth towel in the entire house and tossed them into a laundry basket.

"Hey Mom, can you help me fold this laundry?" Will this work, I wondered?

"Oh, boy, look at all that", she said.

And then, just like a mom, she added, *'Yeah, yeah, bring it over here, I'll get that done.'*

And she did.

And she smiled.

And she felt useful.

And she was happy.

And the morning was rescued.

I swiftly put the puzzle away and she never noticed it was gone.

And then this: I had purchased a child's coloring book of kittens. For toddlers. Clear, easy pictures to color in. I was pleased with myself, thinking she would be able to do this simple activity and we would do it together and I'd play Frank Sinatra music and she would be happy. I whipped it out after breakfast one day, and she looked at it a few minutes. *"This is a book for little children"*, she commented scornfully, pushing the book away. Hmmm. She was right of course.

I bought a coloring book of old movie posters from the 50s and 60s. Not childish at all. She cheerfully colored in *Breakfast at Tiffany's.* First, she commented on all of the flicks she had seen or had not seen. She was stumped by the big crayons though, so I quickly and wordlessly substituted colored pencils. She liked these.

Coloring book of old movie posters? Home run. She had hours of joy coloring in memories from days she could remember.

When Myrtle was successfully occupied, everything worked more smoothly; the day took shape and launched. We did not always cast off smoothly, though. Her skills were an uneven landscape that shifted and disappeared more and more each day.

Sometimes solutions to problems, like soaking false teeth and using lens-less glasses, can be found by relaxing your own grasp on reality. Your loved one lives in an altered state and it won't always resemble a sane one.

Mom had been stripped down to her naked humanity and that is where I tried to meet her; sometimes successfully, sometimes not. I have always preferred orderly and predictable systems. Logic. It was hard to let go of the logic that had mostly ruled my life, but I realized one afternoon that I could choose to feel better about the nonsense talk and chatter, the illogical conversations, and the exhaustion that accompanied a constant pretending. Like Myrtle, I too found comfort in the birds.

Myrtle always watched the birds at the feeder and in the tree branches near her window. They often chattered noisily. *What do you think they are saying to each other?* she asked me dreamily one day. I followed her gaze. I watched the birds closely. They sometimes bobbed their head as they sung. Was it for their own pleasure that they ran through sets of complex harmonics? They often changed their notation so conspicuously that it sounded like improvisation. Is that possible, I wondered? These were smooth meditative runs. Could it be the birds were merely saying, *I am a bird*? No. Not likely, I thought. I replied to Myrt though: *That's a good question, Mom. I wish I knew.*

I could not understand their variations, the lengths of their pauses, the arrangements of their trilling phrases. But it was far too elaborate to be meaningless. I was deeply curious about this but also realized that it was a language I did not know, and that it was a lot like Myrtle's language. My lovely Momma. A sweet flightless bird quavering with a strange song. It is her music now, I thought. Her logic. I don't have to understand it. Like the birds outside her window, she has her own beautiful repertoire. Her birdsong.

As a wounded bird you cry,
But your song was once sweet and dry.
Can I mend your wing and make you sing
And watch you take to the sky?

8
The Big Mistake

At the outset, I thought I could help Myrtle by clarifying and explaining things to her. I thought that maybe, just maybe, I could help her get a grip on reality. I thought that compassion and patience and careful words would do this. One day, Myrtle woke up from an afternoon nap in quite a state. She insisted on knowing where she was. I decided this was my opportunity to make it all very clear to her.

I explained: "You are in New Jersey. You are staying with me now." She stared at me, incredulity in her eyes. So, I continued, "Mom, do you remember the Roxborough Home for Women?"

"Yes", she replied flatly. Surprised by her quick response, but undaunted, I went on: "Okay, well you left there to come here. Now you live here with me!" I finished, cheerfully.

"What? That's impossible!" she cried out. *"My mother and father are looking for me. I have to go home!*

My father is looking for me and he's waiting for me!" She looked positively stricken. I got a bad feeling then, but I was determined to make things clear to her. I distracted her with some coffee and toast, and then sat down to explain more. I fed her facts one at a time, waiting to see if they registered. "Mom, you are 89 years old, do you know this?" She looked a little frightened, but she agreed. I went on slowly and carefully and lovingly. "Mom, if you are 89, that means that your parents are probably well over 100, maybe 110 or 120, right?" I waited, calmly. She looked at me, thoughtfully. *"No. My parents are about 40,"* she said. "But, how can they be 40 if you are 89, Mom?" I asked this in a slow, clear voice. She turned away and looked out of the window.

Then, she began to weep uncontrollably. "What's wrong, Mom?" I did not expect this. I was crestfallen. And stumped.

In between her bitter sobs, she said, *"If I am 89 then my parents are dead. But no one told me. No one told me! That is the worst thing in the world. Who could be so cruel?"* she wailed. Nothing I said could console her. She wept and wept and wept. Myrtle had no memory of her parents' deaths. Although I knew that she had been with them when they died, that part of her brain was forever gone and no amount of clever prodding and careful questioning from me could retrieve this vanished neural real estate. Dementia had taken that memory away forever, and she was left to conclude that their deaths had been hidden from her. Nothing else made sense to her. She concluded that she had been wickedly deceived somehow. She had been robbed of the need to tell her parents that she loved them. She had been cheated; she did not get to say goodbye. This she believed with all her heart and it was a devastating blow.

It was a mistake to try to get her to understand. It was a big mistake. I had not known how poorly this decision would play out. I never forgot it though. I have had to forgive myself many times for my hubris and dense-headed determination on that day. I will continue to forgive myself for it, even now that Myrtle is gone.

I'd never seen my mother cry before dementia. She was the most stoical woman I knew. She was a rock. Now she cried all the time. She cried a lifetime of tears. She cried every single day, sometimes for a few minutes, sometimes for a few hours, and there was very little I could do to stem the tide. I wondered often if it was an old, unnamed sadness that had breached the walls of her soul; or was it new sadness, swelling and spilling from some tiny comprehension of her own suspended consciousness. In other words, was it a clear and present suffering? I will never know. Whenever I reflect on this day and on her overwhelming sadness, I feel white-hot, searing pain in my head and throat and heart.

A year before, I would have described Myrtle's mind as tangled wires, like those eternally knotted up earbuds in every kid's backpack. I knew that a patient hand could lay them straight and smooth them out again. That is what

I tried to do. I learned that no amount of love, kindness or patience could unscramble what was left though.

And I didn't know that those tangled days had been the good days.

On the day of *My Big Mistake* I too went to bed crying. I resolved never to try to untangle things for Myrtle again. My job was not to make her understand. While that might make me feel better, this was not what she needed. All she needed was comfort. She was losing pieces of herself every day. She had become an unwilling time traveler, terrified and confused by the disjointed snapshots of history that dangled precariously in her mind. I am part of that fragile history. Now when she asks me questions or asserts a false timeline, I hold her hand, I kiss her forehead, I tuck the blanket around her knees and I smile at her warmly. Honestly, I do not want to be that disappearing snapshot.

I do not want to vanish into thin air, and I do not let go of her hand.

Think of the nonsense as a beautiful birdsong; it has purpose and meaning that might not be obvious to you, but that doesn't make it meaningless.

Be deliberate with your time away from your loved one. Find some joy of your own. Joy is a habit and a choice. And it is portable. It is a decision within your power to make. Did the golden sun rise to greet you today? Is the apple sweet and crisp? Life is flowing through you and it will keep doing that, whether your loved one has a good day or a bad one.

Life's a beautiful bird
Flying with shadow spell
Of a freedom sealed in a dirge
The footprints of stories to tell.

Okwudili

9
The Blink of an Eye

How quick is the blink of an eye? About 300 milliseconds or a third of a second. And this is the window of time in which a conversation with Myrtle can go from having some meaning to no meaning at all – the blink of an eye.

The hairpin turns from sensibility to absurdity often overwhelm me. My husband and kids think that I have superpowers when it comes to tuning out annoying chatter. They are unanimous in this belief, and maybe it is true. But it is not so with Myrtle. It is impossible for me to hear her speak without listening, although I try.

Sometimes, inexplicably, Myrtle unraveled. I recall one week I did not think I'd survive. She had four consecutive days of mere napping – no real sleep. She spat out her medications. She spat out the food in which I hid the medications. She cried and yelled all day long. She threw things. She yelled for hours throughout the night for no discernible reason. It was as if she decided to tear at the world with all her might for as long as she could.

"...a blink of an eye in itself is nothing. But the eye that blinks, that is something. A span of life is nothing. But the man who lives that span, he is something. He can fill that tiny span with meaning, so its quality is immeasurable though its quantity may be insignificant. Do you understand what I am saying? A man must fill his life with meaning; meaning is not automatically given to life." ~ Chaim Potok

A lot can happen in the blink of an eye. A life can begin or end in that instant. What about that little span between the start and finish? It is everything to us, and it only lasts after we are gone if it held meaning.

I was able to find great comfort in this perspective. Myrtle is still filling her little span. Her milliseconds do not follow any order now. So what? Nor do they have pace. Big deal. She is a special kind of time traveler, that's all. She floats around the milliseconds, living fluidly in the past *and* the present. She can observe the rhododendron petals lost to yesterday's heavy rainfall, and mention the chipmunk stealing the birdseed scattered to the ground by the oversized Blue Jay just minutes before. In this same sentence, she wonders aloud if her father is selling his house and why her brothers haven't visited. Remarkable powers of observation coupled with anachronistic impossibilities. In the same sentence.

Occasionally, she fills the tiny span furiously, as though she just remembered that meaning is not automatically given to life, that we must work at it. She does not rest. She is still adding meaning to her span. That's all.

After these four days of chaotic, living – which did not feel like the blink of an eye – she slept for 24 hours.

She has done many things well. She has done many things right. She packed meaning into all of the nooks and crannies of her life and that is the point of life after all.

It is hard work to fill one's life with meaning.
That I do not think you understand yet.
A life filled with meaning is worthy of rest.
I want to be worthy of rest when I am no longer here.
~Chaim Potok

We are all filling the span that we are given to live; we fill it with meaning moment by moment each day. We do it at ages twenty, fifty and ninety. It helped me to cope when I viewed my mom's periods of agitation as final efforts to do this worthy work. It also made me realize that these were *final* efforts. She was getting weaker and she had entered a stage of disharmony that was much worse. The paradox buried in this end stage of life is that we want to turn away from it. It's not just hard – it's painful to watch. It brings us close to our own vulnerability and mortality. We fear death. Maybe if we stay close, and survive the tempests of the final chapter, we also receive the gift of peacefulness when the end does come. We get to see firsthand that it should not be feared. To temper our fear of death, it helps to get closer.

Birds wing away from
wind and rain and danger
for a better view, it seems.

10
Crying Uncle

Taking care of Myrtle got harder and harder. I was bone-tired every day and the burden on my family was apparent. I was lucky – I had help. I hired a terrific young lady who relieved me regularly for a few hours, and during that time I'd go food shopping or take a run or make an appearance in one of my children's lives. They were 22, 19, 17 and 14 at this time.

It was increasingly clear that I could not keep it up. It was too much. And she had only been with me for ten weeks when I came to this cold hard truth.

Earlier I explained that Myrtle was not suffering from other problems. She did not have heart disease, diabetes, high blood pressure, kidney issues or cancer. She had dementia and only dementia. She was going to die from dementia and it would be slow because that's the way it works. It had already been a decade – a slow decade of decline. Little by little dementia was stealing pieces of her personhood. Little by little she was vanishing before our eyes. When dementia took away her ability to swallow, then it would be a matter of weeks. Myrtle was far from this stage and the weight of her hour-by-hour care had become unbearable. I moved more slowly. I was stooped and my brow was permanently knitted, anticipating the next blow to my heart. I was yanked through the frantic upheavals in her mind and it was exhausting and heartbreaking.

It was around the six-week point that Myrtle became relentlessly belligerent. She became more radically unhinged. She was upset every single day. She wanted to be where all the other old ladies were, she'd say. She would yell for hours, *"I don't want to be in this hotel anymore!"*

Adjustments were made to her meds with no improvement. The job seemed impossible. She was so angry and upset all of the time.

Myrtle began spitting out her meds and clawing her way out of bed in the middle of the night. I could not and would not strap her in, so she did everything in her power to escape. She began rolling out and onto the floor. Getting Myrtle off the floor required the help of EMS staff. When this happened, everyone in the house would be up for hours.

Myrtle was miserable. I had done all that was humanly possible and was facing a limit I didn't know I had. I had massive guilt because I was no longer able to make her happy. She had entered a different stage of dementia – one I could not combat. I had failed.

My siblings and I set about looking for the best place for Mom. Brian found a centrally located home, and although it wasn't cheap, neither was it very expensive. We all agreed she could afford it.

We visited the new place and while it was evident it was not really a place to thrive and recover, there were many plusses. It was mostly women. They were just as far gone as Myrtle. She'd share a room, but her roommate was in her final days, so it would soon be a private room. It had activities and a lovely outdoor patio.

This was the place that Myrtle would die and we all knew it. That made the move one of the saddest days of our lives. Although the day was draped with the heaviness of failure, I did not struggle with the right versus wrong of it. I simply could not take any more and I knew it.

We signed the paperwork and after Myrtle had been with me for twelve weeks, we made her last and final move.

Anger. I saw this in Myrtle more each day. I felt it growing in myself, too. At times this feeling of fury was outpaced only by feelings of failure.

Myrtle, like five million others in the USA, was a prisoner to dementia. I could not change this.

Witnessing her ups and downs was like watching an injured, flightless bird trapped in a room with a hungry house cat.

While we know that cats play with their prey, we do not like to see it happen.

She could not manage the extremes of terror and discouragement and neither could I. This fat, mean cat – this sinister prison warden – would win in the end and I found it helped a bit to acknowledge this. This is not the same thing as giving up and it does not declaw this monster. But it does create a more peaceful spirit for the caregiver. It helps to accept that your role is not to rescue. But you can provide a more loving passage home. You cannot hold back death but you can hold back loneliness. Toward the end, that was all that was left for me to do. Knowing this helped.

You disappeared; I know not where.
But your wing-marks still linger there.
A broken heart cannot fly,
But who decides the time to die?

Delia Owens

11
How Dementia Takes a Life

These have been some of the snapshots leading up to Myrtle's death. Every chapter represents a loss, a setback, a shrinking back from life. This is how old age works and most of us know this and accept it. Dementia is different.

The person we once knew is mostly gone, long before we actually say goodbye. The mysterious *now we see her, now we don't* aspect keeps us in a state of confusion and expectation. It mixes hope with hell.

Then comes the day when hope has vanished and there is only hell. It looks like this, more or less.

They withdraw. They stop trying to make sense of things. Their lives are reduced to one room and usually a bed in that room. The things which could make them smile – a grandchild, a doll, a vase of flowers or a hand massage – these do not have the same effect. These things now fail to pull them out of the darkness into the light.

They eat very little. They drink very little. They don't seem to have the energy for conversation. They do not argue any more. Everything is a trial; every breath appears to be a great effort.

You can see that the effort from your loved one to merely breath and stay alive is too much. She cannot and does not open her eyes. She starts to sleep more and is in and out of consciousness.

No two individuals approach their final days and hours in the exact same way. This is how the end crawled closer and closer for my mom.

First, she forgot little things.

Then, she forgot big things.

After some years, her brain and her body forgot how to stand and walk.

She forgot how to hold her eyes open.

Then, she forgot how to swallow.

Finally, her brain forgot how to breathe. Her brain forgot how to stay alive.

Life's a beautiful bird
Perching in the cobweb of death
In freedom's bond gird
Swaying on the gnaw of time's breath

Okwudili

12
Gone

Myrtle did not have much awareness around this time. When we visited her in her shared room, she was unaware of her roommate, Norma. Two weeks after Myrtle moved in, Norma died. I don't know what was more unnerving – the smell of death in that poor woman's final days as she lay waxen-faced and trapped between life and death, or the fact that no one came to be with her. The facility paid a sitter who watched over the old woman, but she was alone.

Every time I visited during Norma's last days, there was a voice in my head repeating the same words. I will not let Myrtle die like this. God, please don't let it be like this.

There was plenty of activity in Mom's room as supplies were moved out and the space was rearranged for just one occupant – Myrtle. But Myrtle didn't notice any of this. She couldn't notice what was happening around her; it took too much effort.

She declined more rapidly. I blamed myself. Did she get good care at this new place? Yes. No real complaints. Did she get better care in my home? Yes. There is no doubt about that. Could I have kept it up through all of the brutal, final stages and the many weeks these final stages took? No. No, I could not.

We all visited her. My sisters, my brothers and me. Almost every day, one of us was there to sit and hold her hands. I do think she knew we were her children. She definitely felt our love. I know this.

She would cry uncontrollably when we left. She wanted to be touched and held. Every week, often twice a week, when I visited her, I'd wash her hands and her face, brush her hair, put lotion on her. I touched her constantly and I take comfort knowing that she needed this and we gave it to her as often as we could.

Still she withered. She deflated each week. She was barely there. She was unspeakably sad. And so weak. My heart will never be the same, watching death crawl a little closer each day.

I prayed to God to take her with a heart attack, a stroke, something to relieve the soul-crushing losses we had to witness each week. Then I was stricken with guilt for even thinking such a thing.

Within a few months, Myrtle could not swallow. There was simply a day on the calendar when her brain forgot how. The staff tried to offer her yogurt, but she could not swallow it. We used water droppers to keep her as hydrated as possible. Myrtle had a living will. She was very clear in this document. No medical interventions were to be used.

A week after the water dropper feeding began, we got a call from the facility that Myrtle would not wake up – could not wake up – and that we should probably come quickly.

This was not a surprise. We were all on alert and we were visiting as frequently and as long as we could. It was obvious that the end was growing closer, but it was still impossible to imagine it.

Once the call came, I was there in an hour. Brian was there when I arrived. Myrtle was a shadow beneath the sheets. Her breathing was very labored; her chest heaved in great exertion with every inhalation. I wasn't sure if she could hear anything. Probably not. I played her favorite song on my iPhone and placed it by her ear. Doris Day's *Que Sera Sera*. I sat next to her on the bed and held her hand. Brian sat at the foot of the bed. I wondered if she felt pain. I wondered if she was afraid. I watched her closely. She inhaled and exhaled steadily for a few moments and then she simply failed to exhale. I waited and waited but she was still and gone. Just like that. I remember saying "No!" as I looked around the room wondering where she had gone. How could her life be gone? I prayed. I wept. After all that had happened over the years, how could I feel so unprepared and so unwilling to lose her? I wanted her back.

My siblings arrived and we had time to say goodbye. Of course, we had not had our mom for a very long time. But this goodbye was different, because now we all existed on this planet without her. It still doesn't feel right. I don't think it ever will.

I am grateful forever that I got to be with her when she exhaled her last breath. And when I closed my eyes that evening, I imagined my sweet Momma with her new found wings, soaring above me with glee and confidence, a jewel in the heavens, ablaze.

Many people wonder how dementia takes life. This is how it took my mom's life.

I did not want my mom to suffer. I did not want her to linger, but I did not want her to leave either. I'm not sure what I would have changed, if changing mom's ending had even been a choice.

Do we have a right to die with dignity? Yes, I think so. How? I do not know.

So many lives are lost to accidents or evil-doing and these victims don't get to say goodbye; they don't have time to prepare, to forgive, to say thank you. This is unfair.

Does a pronouncement of imminent death lay claim to some special dispensations for how it's going to unfold? Does the knowledge inform the process and endow it with special exceptions?

As heartbreaking as it was to bear witness to Myrtle's death, the only thing about it that was unnatural was that her mind left before her body did. It is this which makes it so hard, because you have all the time in the world to say goodbye to a loved one who is dying of dementia, but there is never really a single moment in all the days, weeks, months and years when there is an awareness substantial enough to take full advantage of this time.

It is a perpetual farewell to a disappearing person.

Dementia does not fight fair. If you understand and accept this at the outset, it will help you forgive yourself the things you cannot do, and be happy for all of the little things you can.

Acknowledgements

Thank you, Daniel, Brian, Kathleen and Susan. I hit the sibling lotto with the four of you. All that could have been made hard, you made easier with your patience and grace. We have been a strong team over these years. Kathleen and Brian, it must be pointed out, you did more than your fair share. I hope you know that we had Mom close to us *longer,* thanks to your enduring efforts. We are all the beneficiaries of something very special – we had a mom who gave us something that she herself had never had. We are so lucky. Thoughts for our father – for the years he never saw and the love he never knew.

Love and deep gratitude for my husband, Peter, who watched me try, watched me succeed, and watched me fail. You never wavered in your complete, unshakeable love and support and you never complained once.

To my four extraordinary children – John, Nora, Andy and James – wellsprings of comfort and love, and my reasons for just about everything. Thank you for always understanding, always loving and always helping.

Finally, this book is for you, Myrtle. You were a wonderful mother. These words will not fill the gap left by your slow flight from this Earth, but they are all I have. They are yours.

Resources

Alzheimer's Foundation www.alzfdn.org

Alzheimer's Association www.alz.org

Dementia Society of America www.dementiasociety.org

National Dementia Association
www.nationaldementia.org

Dementia Bulletin www.facebook.com/dementiainfo/

Dementia Caregivers Support Group
www.facebook.com/groups/672984902717938/

Alzheimer's and Dementia Weekly
www.facebook.com/AlzheimersWeekly/

Dementia Support www.facebook.com/HelpDementia/

Made in the
USA
Middletown, DE

77312137R00056